coffee season

dina ezzeddine

coffee season. Copyright © 2023, 2024 by Dina Ezzeddine. All rights reserved.

No part of this publication may be reproduced, stored in retrieval system or transmitted by any means, electronic, mechanical, photocopying, recording or otherwise written permission of the copyright holder.

Cover Images used under License. Poem: Blossom (A Bouquet) : Edward Smyth Jones

Published by: Kindle Direct Publishing & IngramSpark, and all eBook platforms.
Cover design by: Cauldron Press Book Cover Design

ISBN: 978-1-0688396-0-3   (softcover)
ISBN: 978-1-0688396-1-0   (hardcover)

"Poetry and beauty are always making peace. When you read something beautiful you find coexistence; it breaks walls down."

— Mahmoud Darwish

With Thanks

The wonderful and talented Inessa who created my beautiful book cover. Once again its a pleasure to work with you in creating magic. Thanks to everyone who is reading this book and loves poetry. Grab a coffee or a tea, relax and enjoy!

Contents

01-05
Coffee Season . 1

06-08
Those Who Roam . 1

09-11
Paris, France

12-17
Let's Have Tea. 2

18-21
Those Who Roam . 2

22-24
London, England

Contents

25-29
Cappuccino . 3

30-34
Those Who Roam . 3

35-38
Tokyo, Japan

39-43
Espresso . 4

44-47
Those Who Roam . 4

48-50
Venice, Italy

Contents

51-55
London Fog . 5

56-58
Those Who Roam . 5

59-61
Athens, Greece

62-66
English Breakfast . 6

67-69
Those Who Roam . 6

70-72
Barcelona, Spain

Contents

73-77
matcha tea . 7

78-80
Those Who Roam . 7

81-83
Giza Necropolis, Egypt

84-88
hot chocolate . 8

89-91
Those Who Roam . 8

92-95
Switzerland

Contents

96-100
french vanilla . 9

101-103
Those Who Roam . 9

104-108
Oh Canada!

Coffee Season

coffee season . I

COFFEE TIME

In the quiet morning hours,
I sit with my cup coffee in hand,
Steam rising in gentle tendrils,
The aroma filling the air.

Sipping slowly, savoring each moment,
Time stands still, and I take a breath,
The world outside fades away from life,
And I am left with just me and the comfort of coffee.

Coffee Time, a sacred ritual.
A moment of peace in this chaotic world,
Bittersweet elixir, warming my soul, and heart,
Bringing me back to myself.

I close my eyes and bask in the moment,
The simple pleasure of a quiet morning.
As I sip my coffee in content,
In stillness of this sacred time.

BREATHE!

SPRING

In the soft embrace of Spring's gentle touch,
Nature awakens from its wintry slumber.
The Earth bursts forth in a riot of vibrant colors,
As blossoms bloom and birds fill the air with song.

The trees sway in the warm breeze,
Their branches reaching towards the sun.
The fragrance of blooming flowers, captivates me,
A sweet symphony for the senses to absorb.

The days grow longer, the nights grow shorter,
And the world feels alive once more.
The grass is a lush green carpet of beauty,
Inviting us to kick off our shoes and RUN free.

The sun shines down with a golden grace,
Warming our skin and lifting our spirits.
 Spring is a time of renewal and rebirth,
A season of hope, love, and endless possibilities.

JUST BREATHE!

SUMMER

In the shimmering heat of the summer's embrace,
The sun dances on the horizon with grace,
A symphony of cicadas fills the air,
As time slows down without a care.

The grasses sway in the gentle breeze,
Whispering secrets to the towering trees,
Children laugh and play in the cool stream,
Dreaming sweetly beneath the sunny beams.

As the days stretch long into the starlit night,
Fireflies twinkle in the fading light,
A soft melody of nature's song,
Summer's magic will forever belong.

So let us cherish these moments so rare,
For in the blink of an eye, they'll vanish into thin air,
And we'll be left longing for the days of summer's glow,
When life was simple, and time moved slow.

AUTUMN

The leaves are falling gently to the ground,
A carpet of red, orange, and gold surrounds,
The crisp cool air fills my lungs,
As nature's beauty in AUTUMN has begun.

The trees stand bare, stripped of their leaves,
Their branches reaching for the sky with ease,
The sun sets early, the nights grow long,
Nature's cycle of life and death become a song.

The squirrels scurry, collecting their food,
Preparing for winter, in a frenzied mood,
The birds migrate to warmer lands,
Leaving behind the cold's harsh demands.

Autumn is a time of change and evolution,
A season of reflection, a time for vision,
As we watch the world around us transform,
We are reminded of the beauty of nature's norm.

So let us embrace the autumnal glow,
And let the beauty of the season slowly show,
For in the midst of change and decay,
There is always beauty in the AUTUMN day.

WINTER

In the still silence of winter's embrace,
The world shifts to a hush of frozen grace.
White blankets cover the Earth in armistice,
While icy fingers of frost slowly upsurge.

The trees stand bare and stark against the sky,
Their branches reaching up, up, as if to fly.
The sun hangs low, casting shadows long,
As nature's lullaby sings its winter beautiful song.

The air is crisp and biting cold,
Yet there's a beauty in these days of old.
For in the winter's icy grip,
There lies a sense of wonder, a tranquil journey.

So let us embrace the season's chill,
And find solace in the silence, still.
For winter's beauty likes its a plain embrace,
A reminder of nature's ever-changing grace.

JUST EMBRACE WINTERS GRACE!

Coffee Season

THOSE WHO ROAM . I

INNOCENT WANDERERS

In the shadows of night they roam,
Innocent wanderers seeking a home,
Lost souls drifting in the dark,
Searching for a place to embark.

Their eyes are filled with longing,
Their hearts are heavy with yearning,
They travel far and wide,
In hopes of finding a place to reside.

Through the valleys and through the mountains,
They search for sacred fountains,
Where they can quench their thirst,
And rest their troubles aside.

But the road is long and winding,
And the days are unforgiving,
Yet they press on with determination,
Guided by silent inspiration.

For those who roam are never alone,
Their spirits strong, their hearts grown,
In the face of adversity, they stand tall, and proud,
Innocent wanderers, destined to wander until they're old.

STREET DRIFTERS

On the streets they drift, lost and alone,
Those who roam, in search for a home.
Their footsteps echo in the quiet night,
Their faces hidden from the harsh streetlights.

They carry burdens heavy on their backs,
The weight of the world in their empty sacks.
Their eyes tell stories of struggle and pain,
Their hearts full of longing, for something to gain.

Through alleyways and shadows, they tread,
Their future uncertain, their past filled with dread.
But still they walk, moving forward each day,
Hoping for a better tomorrow or come what may.

For those who roam, the journey is long,
But they are resilient, for they are drifters.
They may be lost, but they are not alone,
For in their hearts, there is a sense of home.

THOSE WHO ROAM

In the stillness of the night,
they wander, aimless and alone.
Lost souls without a guiding light to call home,
those who roam.

Through the darkness, they seek,
answers to questions left unknown.
They walk in silence, never weak, never alone,
for those who roam.

Their footsteps echo in the night,
a haunting melody all their own.
Forgotten dreams take flight,
for those who roam.

In the shadows, they find the calm,
a refuge from a world dethroned.
In their hearts, a silent promise,
for those who roam.

For in their wandering, they discover,
a truth that cannot be outshone.
In the depths of their being, they uncover,
those who roam.

Coffee Season

PARIS, FRANCE

Coffee Season

THE CITY OF LOVE

In the City of Light, where lovers roam
Hand in hand along the white cobblestone
Boulevards lined with cafes and great art
Paris, is a masterpiece of the heart

The Eiffel Tower stands tall and proud
A symbol of love that whispers aloud
From Montmartre to the Seine's gentle flow
Beauty and history at ever Château

The streets come alive with laughter and song
Where dreams take flight and memories belong
Paris, a tapestry of colors and sights
A city of wonder beneath the moonlit nights

In every corner, there is a story to be told
Of passion, of joy, of love so bold
Paris, a canvas of dreams come true
A place where the heart finds its due

So, let us wander, hand in hand
Through the streets of Paris, where we'll stand
A city of love and beauty unbound.
À mon amour Paris, France !

EIFFLE TOWER

In the heart of Paris, a building stands tall,
A monument of love, pride and desire.
The Eiffel Tower, so majestic and grand,
A symbol of beauty to be seen across the land.

Its iron frames reach towards the sky,
A beacon of light that never fades.
Visitors flock from near and far,
To marvel at this tall iconic star.

At night, it sparkles with a dazzling glow,
A sight that takes your breath, will putt on a show.
Romantic couples walk hand in hand,
In the shadow of this towering stand.

Oh Eiffel Tower, you stand so strong,
A reminder that love can never go wrong.
Forever etched in history's page,
A symbol of hope for every age.

TAKE A BREATHE... AND TRAVEL!

À MON AMOUR

In the city of love
Where hearts beat as one
Romance fills the air
Underneath the glimmering sun

Lovers stroll hand in hand
Through cobblestone streets
Whispers of affection
In every corner they meet

The Eiffel Tower stands tall
A symbol of devotion and love
With timeless emotion

Cafés buzz with laughter
As friends share old tales
In this city of veils

But beyond the surface
Lies a heart that beats true
The city of love, of passion and life
Will always welcome you!

Coffee Season

let's have tea . II

THE MORNING RITUAL

In the quiet of the morning light
I sip my tea, feeling soothed with delight
A ritual that brings me peace and joy
As the steam rises, troubles cease

The clink of China, the delicate pour
Savoring each moment, nothing more
Just me and my cup, a simple delight
Tea time is my solace, my respite

The world outside can wait a while
As I let myself unwind and smile
In this moment, I am content
With my tea, my thoughts, my intent

So, I'll cherish this time, precious and few
For tea time brings me back to the true
Simple pleasures, moments of grace
A cup of tea, a quiet place.

BEE'S OF SPRING

Beneath the blossoms, Bee's of Spring take flight
Their buzzing wings, a orchestra filled with delight
Swaying with the petals, they softly land
Sipping sweet nectar, from each gentle pistil

Their dance is graceful, like ballet in the air
Collecting pollen, with such tender care
A harmony of colors, as they flit and sway
Bringing life to gardens, in their own unique way

In tune with nature, in harmony they work
Creating honey, a sweet recipes quirk
Their gentle hum, such a soothing sound
A reminder of the beauty, that can be found

So let us cherish, the Bee's of Spring
For without them, there would be no zing
They bring us joy, in their gentle flight
A reminder of nature's boundless might.

HARMONY OF SUMMER

In a world where chaos reigns,
Harmony is what our spirit craves.
The gentle ebb and flow of life,
Balancing joy and strife.

In harmony we can find our peace,
A music of unity that will never cease.
Like a melody that echoes in our soul,
Bringing comfort and making us whole.

Harmony is the rhythm of life,
The dance of yin and yang, and of dark and light.
It is the thread that weaves us all together,
In a tapestry of love that will last forever.

So let us strive for harmony each day,
In our words, our actions, in our every way.
For in the Harmony of Summer, we find our truest self,
And in this harmony, we find our truest wealth.

ELIXIR OF SUMMER... BREATHE IT IN!

LEAVES OF AUTUMN

In the cool and gentle breeze of autumn,
Fallen leaves dance and twirl,
A kaleidoscope of vibrant colors,
Covering the ground in a rustic swirl.

Each leaf has a story,
Of summer days now gone,
Of the sun-kissed trees they once adorned,
Now withered and alone.

But in their final act of beauty,
They create a carpet so divine,
A tapestry of gold, crimson, and orange,
A majestic sign of nature's design.

So let us pause and admire,
The leaves of autumn's grace,
For they remind us of life's fleeting beauty,
And the seasons' gentle embrace.

THE COLD OF WINTER

The snow falls gently,
Blanketing the world in white.
The air is icy,
Biting at my skin with every breath.

I pull my coat tighter,
Try to shield myself from the cold,
But it seeps right through me,
Settling deep into my bones.

I walk alone in winter,
Footsteps muffled by the snow.
Silent and still
Lost in the cold...

next...

... continued

... the trees stand bare,
And shiver ever so slightly,
Branches reach up, so high to the sky,
Their beauty stark and haunting,
Against the backdrop of white.

But despite the chill,
There is a certain peace,
A stillness that settles,
As the world sleeps.

And though the cold may bite,
And the wind may howl,
I find comfort in the beauty,
Of this Cold Winter's night.

STAY WARM OUTSIDE!

Coffee Season

THOSE WHO ROAM . II

TRAVELERS

We travel through endless roads and open skies,
Our wandering spirit never dies,
Through mountain trails and forests green,
The world's travelers can be seen.

From city lights to sandy shores,
The journey never truly bores,
Strangers are met along the way,
Sharing stories, night, and day.

Traveler's, nomads, souls set free,
Embracing life's diversity,
Seeking truth and seeking peace,
With every mile, their worries cease.

Through deserts hot and icy lands,
They walk with purpose, hearts in hand,
The road ahead is never clear,
But with faith in themselves, there's nothing to fear.

So, here's to those who roam and explore,
For they know what life is truly for,
Travelers, forever wandering lovers.

FAR AWAY LANDS

In the heart of every traveler
Lies a yearning deep and true
To explore the world around them
And discover something new

They wander through bustling cities
And quiet, serene towns
Their feet carry them to distant lands
Where adventure knows no bounds

They seek out hidden treasures
In every corner of the Earth
They chase the sunsets
And marvel at the birth...

next. . .

... continued

... of cultures rich and diverse
That shape the world we see
Travelers are ambassadors
Of curiosity and glee

They leave behind a footprint
In every place they roam
And carry memories with them
That make the world their home

So, here's to all the travelers
Who venture near and far
May their journeys be fulfilling
And their wanderlust never bar.

Coffee Season

ANCIENT CITY OF RUINS

In lands far away, where dreams take flight,
Where the sun sets in hues of golden light,
There lies a world unknown to me,
Where mountains touch the sky, and the sea is free.

Fields of Emerald green, and skies of blue,
Where the wind whispers secrets, old and new,
In these far away lands, my heart longs to roam,
To find a place that feels like home.

In cities of bustling streets and ancient ruins,
Where history whispers in forgotten tunes,
I yearn to explore, to learn and to see,
What wonders awaits in lands far from me.

Through valleys and rivers, forests, and plains,
I'll journey on, through sunshine and rain,
For in these far away lands, I'll find my soul,
And in their beauty, I'll find myself whole.

Coffee Season

LONDON, ENGLAND

IN THE HEART OF LONDON

In London Town, where history breathes
Old stones whisper secrets of yesteryears
Streets alive with the rhythm of urban beats
Echoes of footsteps on cobblestone streets.

From Tower Bridge to the London Eye
The city skyline stretches far and wide
Parks and gardens, a peaceful retreat
Amidst the hustle and bustle of busy streets.

The Thames flows with steady grace
Dividing the city with a watery embrace
Museums and galleries, a feast for the eyes
Art and culture in every corner lie.

From Camden Market to Covent Garden
The city buzzes with vibrant energy
A melting pot of cultures simmer
London, England, a city of dreams.

So, wander through its winding lanes
Explore its nooks and crannies, and hidden alleys
For London Town, the past and present meet
In a timeless dance, forever sweet.

TURKISH DELIGHT

In the heart of London,
Turkish delights abound,
Sugary sweet treats,
In every corner, they can be found.

Rosewater and pistachio are one of a kind,
Melting on your tongues,
A taste of Istanbul,
In a bustling city, so young.

Handcrafted and delicate,
Each piece a work of art,
A culinary masterpiece,
That warms the young at heart.

Turkish Delight in London,
A taste of tradition and pride,
Bringing joy and delight,
To all who takes a bite.

BIG BEN

In the Heart of London town,
Stands a tower tall and proud.
Big Ben, its name renowned,
Marking time with every sound.

Chimes echoing through the night,
Guiding ships in the moon's dim light.
A symbol of strength and might,
Standing firm through every plight.

Time marches on, never stands still,
But Big Ben stands, a steady will,
A guardian of London's thrill,
Watching over the city, tranquil and still.

Coffee Season

cappuccino.III

CAPPUCCINO

In the bustling cafe, I sit
Sipping on my warm cappuccino
The frothy foam tickles my lips
A comforting hug in a cup

The aroma dances around me
A rich blend of coffee and cream
Each sip awakening my senses
Bringing a sense of calm

I watch the world go by
As I lose myself in the creamy swirls
The bitter sweetness melting away
All my worries and doubts

As I finish the last drop
I am left with a feeling of contentment
Ready to face the day ahead
With a cappuccino in my heart.

IT'S SPRING AGAIN

In the air, a gentle warmth returns
As nature awakens from its slumber
The flowers bloom, the birds sing
It's spring again, a time of wonder

The cherry blossoms paint the trees
In shades of pink and white
The grass is green, the sky is blue
It's a truly breathtaking sight

The sun shines brighter, the days grow long
And all around, new life is found
It's spring again, a season of hope
A time to let go of winter's frown

So, let's embrace the beauty of this time
And let our hearts be light
For its spring again, a time for growth
A time for everything to be just right.

IT'S SPRING AGAIN!

IT'S SUMMER AGAIN

In the golden glow of summer's light,
The world awakens, blooms in sight.
The days are long, the nights are warm,
An invitation to embrace the calm.

The sun-kissed days are filled with laughter,
Children's voices ring, ever after.
A gentle breeze rustles through the trees,
Carrying whispers of dreams and ease.

The scent of flowers fills the air,
A symphony of colors everywhere.
The world is alive with endless beauty,
A season of joy a welcomed duty.

Summer has returned once again,
A promise of joy, a gentle friend.
So let us bask in its warmth and light,
And cherish each moment, all so bright.

SUMMER HAS RETURNED... ONCE AGAIN!

IT'S FALL

In the aftermath of summer's blaze,
The world begins to change,
Leaves turn from green to gold,
As the air grows crisp and cold.

An amber hue paints the sky,
As nature prepares to say goodbye,
The trees shed their leaves with grace,
But in this season of letting go,
There is beauty in the ebb and flow.

As the days grow shorter and the nights grow long,
We find solace in nature's song,
For in the falling leaves and cooling breeze,
We find peace in the changing of the trees.

So let us embrace this season of transition,
And find beauty in its repetition,
For in the cycle of rise and fall,
We find strength in embracing it all.

THE CALM OF WINTER

In the quiet stillness of winter's embrace,
The world is wrapped in a blanket of grace.
Snowflakes fall gently, like whispers from above,
Blanketing the Earth in a blanket of love.

The trees stand tall, their branches bare,
Silent sentinels in the frosty air.
The rivers, frozen solid, glistens and gleams,
Reflecting the sun's warm, golden beams.

The animals hibernate, in peaceful response,
Dreaming sweet dreams as the cold doesn't stop.
The world is at rest, in a tranquil lull,
As winter's calm settles the hum.

In this season of quiet, of peace and calm,
We fin solace and comfort in the still beyond.
For in the calm of winter, we find our place,
And feel the beauty of nature's grace.

Coffee Season

THOSE WHO ROAM . III

ROAMERS

In the quiet stillness of winter's embrace,
In the city streets they wander,
Roamers seeking something more,
Their hearts are full of wonder,
Their feet are never sore.

They chase the setting sun,
And dance in the cool nights air,
Their lives are filled with fun,
They have no time to spare.

Roamers of the open road,
With eyes that yearn to see,
Their stories still untold,
Their spirits wild and free...

next...

... continued

... they live life on their terms,
No boundaries to confine,
Their hearts forever burn,
With a restless, wandering mind.

Roamers of the world unite,
In search of truth and bliss,
Their souls are filled with light,
Their journey never missed.

So let us roam with them,
And chase our dreams so true,
For in the end, we'll find,
The wanderer in me and you.

AWAY FROM HOME

In the hustle and bustle of the city streets,
I find consolation in the rhythm of my feet.
Each step a beat, each turn a new melody,
As I wander aimlessly, feeling free.

The streetlights flicker, casting shadows on the pavement,
Car horns blare, creating a chaotic arrangement,
But amidst the noise and the chaos around,
I find a sense of harmony that can't be found.

The city comes alive at night,
With the neon signs shining bright.
The smells of street food fill the air,
As I navigate the urban thoroughfare.

I pass by strangers, each with a story to tell,
Their faces illuminated by the city's spell.
Some lost in thought, some lost in time,
I wonder what adventures they've left behind.

As I walk down these familiar streets,
I feel a sense of belonging, a sense of peace.
The city may be loud and full of strife,
But in its chaos, I find beauty in life.

WONDERLAND

In a world full of wonder and delight,
Where the mountains kiss the sky,
And the oceans stretch out wide and bright,
There's no reason to stay confined, oh why?

Pack your bags and leave your worries behind,
For the open road awaits your restless feet,
With each new place, a treasure to find,
Feel the rush of adventure, oh so sweet.

Explore the towns and cities unknown,
Meet new people, hear their stories unfold,
Let the roads guide you, let your spirit be shown,
For in travel, memories are made of gold.

So, get out and travel, let your heart soar,
Embrace the world, let your wanderlust roar.

ADVENTURE AROUND EVERY CORNER

In the cool breeze of morning,
Let's go on an adventure,
To where the misty mountains lick the sky,
And rivers flow with laughter.

Through lush green valleys,
And forests thick with mystery,
We'll wander aimlessly,
In search of hidden treasure.

Let's chase the setting sun,
As it paints the sky in hues of gold,
And watch as the stars come out to play,
In a dance of beauty untold.

So, take my hand, my dear,
And let's set out on this journey,
For in the magic of this world,
We'll find the greatest of all discoveries.

Coffee Season

TOKYO, JAPAN

TOKYO

City never sleeps
Tokyo lights shine all night
Bustling streets below

Coffee Season

LAND OF THE RISING SUN

Land of the Rising Sun
Golden light on mountains high
New day has begun

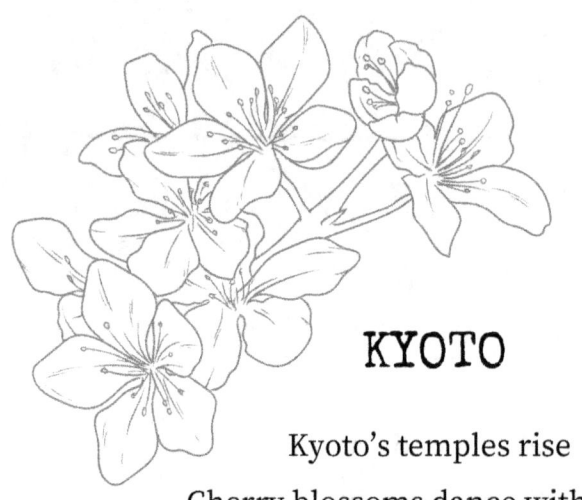

KYOTO

Kyoto's temples rise
Cherry blossoms dance with grace
Ancient beauty shines

OSAKA

Cherry blossoms fall
In Osaka's ancient streets
Beauty blooms always

Coffee Season

espresso . IV

ESPRESSO

In the early morning light
The steam rises from the machine
Prepping for my morning caffeine

The aroma fills the air
Rich and intense, it beckons me near
I pour the shot without any care
Watching as the espresso foams

Dark and velvety, a work of art
The first sip awakens my senses
A jolt of energy to start
My day, no pretense

Espresso, my morning love
Bold and strong, yet smooth and refined
In its presence, I find peace and unity
A moment of calmness, a moment of mine.

THE BEGINNING

In the quiet hours of morning,
Spring whispers softly to the world.
The air is warm, the sky is crisp,
And nature's beauty is unfurled.

The trees are budding, flowers bloom,
Life awakens from its winter gloom.
Birds sing melodies of joy,
As the Earth is filled with wonder.
Life begins anew.

The sun shines bright, the grass is green,
A new beginning is near.
Hope and renewal fill the air,
As spring has finally declared... I AM HERE!

So let us embrace this season again,
With gratitude and love in our hearts.
For spring has begun once more,
And a fresh new journey starts.

LIVE, LAUGH, LEARN!

THE BEACH

Upon the sandy shores of the beach

Where the waves crash and the seagull's screech

A sense of peace and calm I seek

As the sun slowly starts to bleach

The salty air fills my lungs

And the sound of the oceans begins to hum

I feel like I've just begun

To let go of all of life's burdens

The sand beneath my toes so warm

As I watch the pelicans preform

Diving into the water, with graceful form

Nature's beauty, so wild and untamed

I close my eyes, feeling the breeze

And let all my worries release

In this moment, I am truly at ease

At one with the ocean, at one with the beach.

THE END OF SUMMER

As summer fades, leaves turn to gold
Autumn whispers secrets untold
A chill in the air, a hint of change
Nature's beauty, ever so strange

The end of warmth, the start of cool
Crunching leaves, like a playful fool
The sun sets earlier, the nights grow long
A melancholy feeling, a bittersweet song

But with every end comes a new start
A fresh beginning, a beating heart
Fall comes alive in vibrant hues
An orchestra of reds, oranges, and blues

So, embrace the shift, the receding tide and flow
Let go of summer, let autumn show
The beauty in change, in letting go
For in every ending, a new chapter will grow.

What will yours be and how will you know!

THE CALM

The frozen tundra of a cold winter's night
Lies silent, still and stark
Snow-covered plains stretch endlessly
In a blanket of white, cold, and dark

The trees stand bare, with branches reaching
Towards a starlit sky so clear
The moon shines bright, casting shadows
On the icy ground around you

The air is crisp, with a biting chill
That cuts through marrow and bone
But in the frozen wasteland
I find a beauty all its own

For in the stillness of the night
I hear a whisper soft and light
The tundra speaks of ancient tales
Of creatures fierce and mountain hale

So, I stand in awe of this frozen land
And offer up a prayer
For the tundra of a cold winter's night
Is a world so pure and rare.

Coffee Season

THOSE WHO ROAM . IV

THOSE IN ROME

Upon the ancient streets,
Wanderers in Roam travel freely.
Lost in the echoes of history,
Their souls connected to the past.

They meander through ruins,
Whispers of empires long gone.
In the shadow of the Colosseum,
They feel the weight of time.

Through the bustling piazzas,
They breathe in the essence of the city.
Each step a dance,
Each corner a mystery.

Those in Rome are wanderers,
Seekers of truth and life.
They are poets without words,
Artists without a canvas.

In the heart of this eternal city,
They find themselves lost and found.
Guided by the spirits of the ancients,
They are forever wandering.

WHEN IN SPAIN

In Spain, where travelers roam
Through streets of history and of stone
The sun shines bright, the tapas flow
As they explore, feelings start to grow

From Barcelona to Sevilla's square
The beauty of culture fills the air
With flamenco rhythms, castanets click
Each step they take, a new chapter to pick

In Madrid's bustling streets they find
A blend of old and modern intertwined
The art and architecture, oh so grand
A feast for the eyes, on every hand

Through markets and cafes, they wander free
Immersed in a world, so rich in history
The spirit of Spain, alive and strong
In every corner, where they belong

So come, oh travelers, embrace the sights
Let Spain's magic fill your nights
In this land of passion and grace
May your adventures leave a lasting trace.

Coffee Season

THE CITY THAT NEVER SLEEPS

In the city that never sleeps

Neon lights flicker and dance

Like fireflies in the night sky

Echoes through the streets

The hustle and bustle never ends

As cars honk and people rush

To catch a train or take the bus

In this concrete jungle

Where dreams are made and broken...

next . . .

... continued

... the city pulses with energy
A cacophony of sounds
From sirens to street performers
And the night holds endless promise

In the city that never sleeps
I find solace in the chaos
A small speck in a vast expanse
Yet somehow connected
To teach soul and share this space

So, I embrace the madness
And let it carry me away
In the heart of this vibrant city
That never truly rests
But keeps us alive and inspired.

Coffee Season

VENICE, ITALY

THE GONDOLAS

In Venice, Italy where the waters flow
Gondolas glide with a gentle row,
Buildings rise from the sea's embrace,
A city of beauty, and timeless grace.

Canals crisscross through ancient streets,
Tourists wander, their hearts yet to meet,
The charm of a place that captures the soul,
In Venice, Italy where dreams unfold.

From St. Mark's Square to the Doge's Palace,
History whispers in every place,
Art and culture intertwine,
In this city where the sun always shines.

As the sunset paints the sky hues of gold,
Venice's beauty never grows old,
A magical place, filled with art and song,
In Venice, Italy, is where you belong.

THE DISAPPEARING CITY

In Venice, Italy, the city of dreams
Canals and gondolas, a water wonderland it seems
But beneath the beauty lies a deeper truth
This city is vanishing, fading from our view.

As the water rises, the buildings decay
Venice is sinking, day by day
Tourists flock to see the sights
But few stop to ponder the city's plight.

The grand palaces and cathedrals tall
Will one day be underwater, lost to all
The disappearing city, a tragic fate
As we watch helplessly, standing at its gate.

Venice, Italy, a treasure to behold
But its future is uncertain, its story untold
We must cherish and protect this frail place
Before it disappears without a trace.

LOVE BLOOMS

In the city of Venice, Italy
Where my lover and I went
Strolling hand and hand
Through narrow streets and winding canals

The gondolas gliding gracefully
Beneath the bridges we walked
Past ancient buildings soaked in history
And the aroma of freshly baked bread

We gazed at the grandeur of San Marco
And sipped espresso in quaint cafes
Lost in the labyrinth of alleys
Getting lost in each other's eyes

In this magical city of love
Where time seems to stand still
We found a piece of heaven
In each other's arm, we found our thrill

Venice, where romance blooms
In every cobblestone street we roam
Forever etched in our hearts
A love story that's uniquely our own.

Coffee Season

london fog . V

LONDON FOG

In the heart of London, England,
Where the fog rolls in without a sound,
There's a drink that warms the soul,
A remedy for the cold that takes its toll.

London fog, in a cup so warm,
A blend of tea, milk, and vanilla charm,
It soothes the spirit, calms the mind,
A perfect elixir for all who mind.

Themselves lost in the misty haze,
Seeking comfort in these dreary days,
So, raise your cup, to the London fog,
A taste of serenity, that can't go wrong.

THE SEASON OF BIRDS

In the morning light, they begin to sing
Spring birds, their melodies they bring
A music of hope, a chorus of joy
As they flit and flutter, without any ploy

Their feathers gleam in the sun
Their songs a reminder that winter is done
They dance on the breeze with grace
Bringing a smile to everyone's face

Their music fills the air
A reminder that life is fair
They remind us to cherish each day
And to let our worries drift away

So, let us listen to the Spring Bird's song
And let their beauty heal us, all day long
For in their presence, we find peace
And all our troubles seem to cease.

SUMMER MOSQUITO'S

On summer nights, the buzzing begins
As the sun fades and darkness settles in
Tiny vampires in the humid air
Feasting on bare skin without a care

Their high-pitched whine a haunting sound
As they circle around and around
Searching for a patch of flesh to bite
To pierce and feed, causing a red, itchy fight

We swat and slap, trying to defend
Against their relentless and insistent blend
Of annoyance and discomfort, they bring
With each tiny, bloodthirsty sting

But despite our efforts, they persist
Their numbers seemingly never deplete or resist
A reminder that even in the beauty of summer
Nature's creatures can be quite the bummer

So, we arm ourselves with bug spray
And hope for a cooler, mosquito-free day
But until then, we'll just have to endure
The summer mosquitos, and their relentless allure.

HIBERNATION

In the quiet of autumn,
Nature begins to slow,
Leaves falling gently to the ground,
A peaceful, tranquil show.

The animals prepare for a rest,
As winter approaches near,
Hibernation soon to come,
A time of solitude and cheer.

The world around us grows still,
As we cozy up inside,
Embracing the warmth of home,
Finding comfort in the tide.

Autumn hibernation has arrived,
A time to heal and mend,
Before the world wakes up again,
And we begin anew, my friend.

THE RINK

Winter skating brings a thrill
As blades glide on ice so chill
Beneath the sky so bright and clear
We skate without a single fear

The cold air nips at our skin
But we keep on, with joy within
The sound of blades against the ice
Is like a sweet and soothing lullaby

We twirl and spin with grace
In this magical, icy space
Our worries melt away like a snowy day
And we glide on ice, for a hockey game

Winter skating is a joy divine
A chance to escape, a chance to unwind
So, let us glide on this icy rink
And savor every moment, as we skate and think.

Coffee Season

THOSE WHO ROAM . V

THE NIGHT OWLS

In the darkness they roam,
Travelers are wanderers in the night,
Their souls yearning for the unknow,
Their dreams taking flight.

Through cities and towns, they tread,
Seeking out new sights,
With hearts open and minds unfed,
They brace the lonely nights.

Their footsteps echo in the quiet,
Their shadows dance in the moonlight,
Their spirits wild and bright,
Travelers are wanderers in the night.

So they move from place to place,
Chasing the elusive light,
With adventure in their embrace,
Travelers are wanderers in the night.

TAKE A TRIP TO AN UNKNOWN LAND

Step outside your home and travel
Feel the wind against your skin
Let your feet guide you

Through streets line with stories
And sidewalks etched with memories
Discover the beauty of the world

In the laughter of children playing
And the whispers of lovers sharing secrets
In the chatter of birds and the rustle of leaves

Let the sunlight touch your face
And the rain cleanses your soul
Embrace the unknown

For beyond your doorstep lies
A world waiting to be explored
Step outside your home and travel.

TO THE FOREST WE GO

To the forest we go, where shadows dance,
and whispers of ancient tales fill the air
The trees reach up to the sky
their leaves rustling in a soft, gentle sigh

Moss-covered rocks and winding streams
lead us deeper into this magical dream
Birds sing sweet melodies high above
as we wander through this world we love

Through dappled light and darkened glades
we journey on, with hearts unafraid
To the forest we go, to find our peace
and in its embrace, our souls release.

Coffee Season

ATHENS, GREECE

ANCIENT CITY

In the heart of Greece lies, ATHENS
A city of history, art, and beauty
Where ancient ruins stand tall
And modern buildings reach for the sky

The Acropolis watches over the city
A symbol of strength and endurance
As the Parthenon gleams in the sunlight
A reminder of the past's grandeur

Streets filled with bustling markets
And cafes serving delicious cuisine
The sounds of laughter and music
Echo through the narrow alleys

The people of ATHENS are proud
Of their heritage and traditions
Their passion of life is contagious
And their love of their city unwavering

So next time you find yourself in ATHENS
Take a moment to soak it all in
The history, the culture, the spirit
And let yourself be swept away.

ACROPOLIS

In the heart of Ancient Greece,
Stands a marvel of history,
The Acropolis, a symbol of power and grace.

High above the city,
Its columns reach towards the sky,
A testament to a civilization long passed by.

The Parthenon, a temple of Athena,
Stands proud and strong,
Guarding over the land it has watched.

But time has not been kind,
The ruins are weathered and worn,
Yet still they stand, a reminder of a time long gone.

The Acropolis, a beacon of civilization once was,
A testament to the ingenuity of mankind,
A place where history and beauty intertwine.

ATHENA

In the heart of Athens, she reigns
Goddess of wisdom, war and grace
Athena, born of Zeus's mind
Mighty and wise, strong, and kind

With eyes that see beyond mere sight
She watches over warriors at night
A shield and spear by her side
In battles fierce, she will abide

But not just war does she inspire
In arts and crafts, she lights the fire
A patron of knowledge and the arts
She guides humanity in all its parts

So, let us honor Athena's name
In her wisdom, we find our aim
With grace and strength, we face the day
In her guidance, we find our way.

Coffee Season

english breakfast . VI

ENGLISH TEA

In the quiet morning hush
I sip on my English Breakfast tea
The warmth of the mug in my hands
Bringing comfort to me

The rich and robust flavor
Awakens my senses
As the golden liquid flows
Bringing calmness and pretenses

Of a simpler time
Where worries fall away
And all that matters
Is the start of a brand new day

So I savor each sip
As the world begins to wake
English Breakfast tea
A soothing escape.

SPRING SONGS

In the heart of springtime's melody,
the earth awakens from its wintry sleep.
Birds sing in harmony,
flowers bloom and creatures creep.

The sun shines brighter,
warming the land and sky.
A symphony of color,
as the days pass by.

The fields burst with life,
the trees sway in the breeze.
Nature's grand spectacle,
a sight to behold and seize.

Oh, springtime's song,
so sweet and pure.
A reminder of hope,
and the world's enduring allure.

SUMMER TREATS

Beneath the blazing sun's warm embrace,
Summer treats beckon with promises of sweet escape.
Ice cream cones dripping with delightful flavors,
Popsicles so cold they send shivers in ripples and quivers.

Juicy watermelons bursting with summer's essence,
Picnics filled with laughter and silly nonsense.
Lemonades and iced teas to cool the fiery heat,
S'mores by the campfire where friends and family meet.

The taste of summer lingers on our lips,
A fleeting moment of pure bliss.
Memories made in the golden sun,
Summer treats, never to be outdone.

BLOSSOM

A blossom pink, a blossom blue,
Make all there is in love so true.
'Tis fits, methinks, my heart to move.
To give it thee, sweet person, I love!
Now, take it, dear, this morn to wear.
A wrath of beauty in thy hair.
Think on it, when from bliss we part-
The emblem of my wooing heart!

– EDWARD SMYTH JONES

(author note- I love this poem and wanted to include it within this book to give the book a feel of love, warmth and happiness.

THE COLD HAS COME AGAIN

In the quiet stillness of winter's embrace,
The world falls silent, wrapped in icy lace.
The trees stand bare against the cold,
Their branches reaching up to hold,
The weight of snow so pure and white.
A blanket covering the Earth, so bright.

The air is crisp, the sky is clear,
As winter whispers in your ear.
The crunch of snow beneath your feet,
A sound so soft, so pure, so sweet.
The sun sets early, the nights grow long,
But in the darkness, we find a song.

A song of hope, of peace, of rest,
As we snuggle close, feeling blessed.
For in the winter's chill and frost,
We find a warmth we thought was lost.
So let us cherish this fleeting time,
As winter's beauty is so sublime.

Coffee Season

THOSE WHO ROAM . VI

ROAMERS WHO TRAVEL IN THE NIGHT

In swirling skies of endless blue,
Traveling roamers, are fearless and true.
Explorers of lands far and wide,
With hearts open, nowhere to hide.

Through mountains high and valleys deep,
They wander on, without souls to keep.
Seeking wonders, embracing the unknown,
Their spirits wild, like seeds in wind-blown.

From bustling cities to silent shores,
Traveling roamers, forever explorers.
Their journey never-ending, in their path untamed,
In search of truth, not for fame.

They walk with purpose, with passion unfold,
Their story written in stars, in tales of old.
Traveling roamers, nomads of the heart,
Forever free, never apart.

THE GREAT ESCAPE

In the dead of night,
under the cover of darkness,
we plotted our daring escape.

We slipped through the shadows,
silent as ghosts,
our hearts pounding inside.

The walls of our prison,
both physical and mental,
loomed high above us.

But we knew we had to break free,
to taste the sweet air of freedom,
once more, away at night.

With each step,
we left our troubles behind,
our souls lightening with each mile,
covered.

And as we reached the edge of the world,
we looked back at where we had been,
and knew that we were finally truly alive.

THE NIGHT NOMAD

In the darkness of night, the nomad roams
An explorer of the land's unknown
His heart yearning for the next adventure
Guided by the stars above, he wanders

Through forgotten lands and ancient ruins
He finds solace in the silence of the night
The moonlight illuminating his path
As he travels on, is spirit takes flight

No destination in sight, just the open road
The night nomad seeks freedom and solitude
A wanderer without a home, he finds peace in the unknown
For in the darkness of the night, he feels truly alive

With every step, he leaves his mark on the world
A fleeting presence, a whisper in the night
But for the night nomad, that is enough
To know he is truly free.

Coffee Season

BARCELONA SPAIN

BARCELONA

In Barcelona's vibrant streets,

Where the sun kisses the cobblestones,

Artistic expression breaks free,

In every corner, in every nook on the streets,

Gaudi's whimsical masterpieces,

Stand tall against the sky,

Sagrada Familia's spires reaching high,

A testament to perseverance and faith,

A rhythm of flamenco echoes,

Through the hearts of the people,

Tapas and wine flow freely,

As laughter fills the air,

In Barcelona, where the past meets the present,

And the future shines bright,

A city filled with passion and beauty,

Never ceasing to amaze.

BUSTLING CITIES OF SPAIN

In the heart of Europe lies a land of rich history,
Where Moorish castles stand proud and free,
Spain, a place of vibrant culture and tradition,
Where flamenco dances stir the soul with passion.

From the bustling streets of Madrid,
To the sunny beaches of the Mediterranean grid,
Spain enchants visitors with diverse beauty,
From the snow-capped mountains to the azure sea.

The tapas are savory, the wine flows like a river,
And the bullfights draw crowds with adrenaline shivers,
But beyond the tourist attractions and flamboyant displays,
Lies a country with a deep-rooted sense of grace.

The art of Picasso, the music of Gaudi,
The architecture of Dali, all tell a story,
Of a nation that embraces creativity and flair.

So raise a glass to Spain, the land of the fiestas and fun,
Where the sun always shines, and the party's never done,
In this magical place where history and modernity meet,
Spain will forever hold a special place in my heart.

THE ART OF SPAIN

In the heart of Spain,
Where art and passion intertwine,
Eternal beauty captured in every stroke,
The colors of the land come alive.

From Gaudi's whimsical architecture,
To Velazquez's masterful brushstrokes,
Each masterpiece tells a story,
Of love, of war, of life itself.

In sun-drenched streets and hidden alleys,
The spirit of Spain is preserved in art,
A celebration of culture and tradition,
A testament to the human heart.

So let us wander through galleries,
And marvel at the works on display,
For in the art of Spain we find,
A reflection of our own souls at play.

Coffee Season

matcha tea . VII

CERMONIAL TEA
Emerald green tea

Whisked to frothy perfection

Matcha bliss, sip slow

MATCHA PERFECTION
Green tea perfection

Matcha powder melts in a cup

Zen in every sip

MATCHA DELIGHT
Green powder swirling

Matcha's taste so sweet and pure

Peaceful sips delight

SPRINGTIME'S EMBRACE

In springtime's gentle embrace,
Nature awakens with grace.
Blossoms bloom in hues of light,
Birds sing melodies in delight.

The air is filled with sweet perfume,
As flowers dance in full bloom.
The sun shines with golden rays,
Warming souls in joyful displays.

Trees sway with a gentle breeze,
Whispering secrets through the leaves.
Life bursts forth in vibrant array,
In springtime's enchanting display.

A season of rebirth and renewal,
A time of hope and revival.
In spring's embrace, we find delight,
As nature awakens in full flight.

SUMMER'S GRACE

Under the golden sun's warm embrace,
Summer's grace unfurls with gentle pace.
A symphony of buzzing bees and chirping birds,
Whispers of a breeze, carrying sweet-scented words.

The world awakens with a vibrant hue,
A canvas painted with skies so blue.
Fields of green stretch endlessly,
Nature's beauty captured effortlessly.

Days filled with laughter and leisure,
Nights alive with starry treasure.
The season of sun-kissed skin and bare feet,
Where worries fade and hearts beat.

Bask in the glow of summer's grace,
Embrace the joy in every embrace.
For fleeting is this magical time,
Cherish each moment, let it shine.

THE HEART OF AUTUMN

In the heart of autumn's embrace,

The trees whisper their final goodbye,

Leaves rustle and dance in the wind,

A symphony of colors, crimson and gold.

The air is crisp and cool,

As nature prepares for winter's sleep,

The sky is painted with hues of orange and pink,

As the sun sets on another day.

In the heart of autumn's beauty,

We find solace in the changing of the seasons,

A time for reflection and gratitude,

For the abundance that surrounds us.

So let us embrace the magic of fall,

And let our hearts be filled with awe,

For in the heart of autumn's embrace,

We find peace and love once more.

THE EARTH STANDS STILL

The Earth stands still in winter,
A frozen silence blankets the land.
Trees stripped bare of their leaves,
Whispers of the past season linger.

No birds chirp in the cold air,
Only the howling wind can be heard.
The ground is hard and unyielding,
As if nature itself holds its breath.

But beneath the icy surface,
Life still pulses, waiting to emerge.
Seeds sleep in the dark earth,
Dreaming of the warmth to come.

Winter may be harsh and unforgiving,
But it is a necessary pause.
A time for reflection and renewal,
Before the Earth bursts forth in bloom.

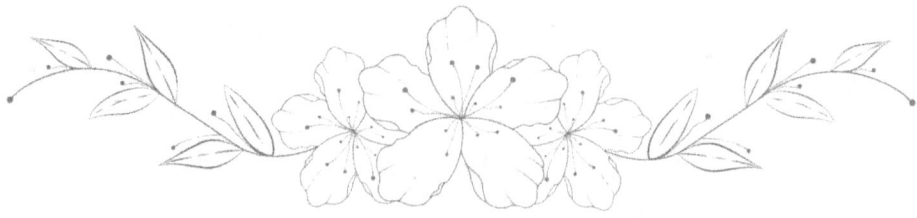

Coffee Season

THOSE WHO ROAM . VII

TO TRAVEL, OH TO LIVE!

In the vast world we roam

To travel, to explore

To see the beauty unknown

And unlock new doors

A journey of self-discovery

A path of endless wonders

Each step a new story

A chance to break free from the thunder

To travel is to be alive

To feel the pulse of the earth

To see the truth that lies

In every corner, every birth

So pack your bags and go

Embrace the unknown

For in travel, we grow

And in new places, we find home

LEAVE BEHIND THE FAMILIAR

To travel oh to live,
To wander and explore.
To leave behind the familiar,
And open new doors.

To breathe in different air,
To see with different eyes.
To learn from every moment,
And let the soul arise.

To feel the heartbeat of a city,
To taste the flavors of a land.
To dance with strangers in the night,
And walk hand in hand.

To travel oh to live,
To find oneself in the journey.
To embrace the unknown,
And let the heart be free.

HEARTBEAT OF A CITY

In the heart of the city,
Where the buildings reach for the sky,
And streets bustle with life,
There is a rhythm that never dies.

It is the heartbeat of the city,
Pulsing with energy and light,
A constant thrum that never falters,
Through the day and into the night.

The city breathes with a life of its own,
Each person a note in its symphony,
The laughter, the cries, the hustle and bustle,
All blending into a beautiful cacophony.

So let your heart beat with the city,
Feel its pulse and its power,
For in its endless rhythm,
You'll find a place to call home.

Coffee Season

GIZA NECROPOLIS, EGYPT

THE PYRAMIDS

In the land of ancient sands
Rise the monuments grand
Giza Necropolis in Egypt
Where history and mystery intertwine

Pyramids towering high
Guardians of the past
Whispers of pharaohs
In the desert vast

Sphinx with lion's gaze
Ancient riddle to unravel
Silent witness to the ages
In the shadows of time's travel

Tombs and temples
Stories cared in stone
Echoes of a civilization
Long gone, yet not alone

Giza Necropolis in Egypt
A sacred place of wonder
Where the past speaks in silence
And the sands keep its secret under

THE ANCIENT PYRAMIDS

In the golden desert sands they stand,
Monuments of a distant past,
The ancient pyramids rise grand,
Majestic structures built to last.

Mystery shrouds their hidden depths,
Whispers of long-forgotten kings,
The secrets kept within their steps,
Echoes of the ancient wings.

Pyramids of power and might,
Testaments to human skill,
An enigma in the desert light,
A vision that time cannot take.

Silent guardians of ages gone by,
Witnesses to a lost civilization,
Majestic against the azure sky,
A symbol of mankind's dedication.

The ancient pyramids still inspire,
Awe and wonder in our hearts,
A legacy that will never tire,
As timeless as the desert's arts.

QUEEN OF THE NILE

In the land of ancient Egypt,

She ruled with grace and power,

The Queen of the Nile, renowned and revered.

With beauty that enchanted all who beheld her,

And intelligence that surpassed even the wisest scholars,

She led her people with wisdom and strength.

Her name echoed through the ages,

A legend that will never fade,

The Queen of the Nile, eternal and unyielding.

Her legacy lives on in the sands of time,

A symbol of strength and resilience,

The Queen of the Nile, forever enshrined in history.

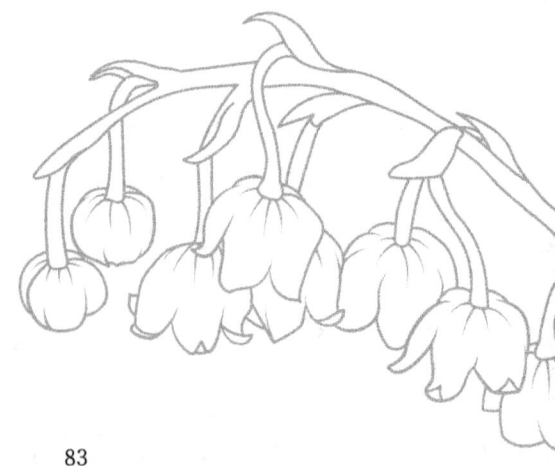

Coffee Season

hot chocolate . VIII

HOT CHOCOLATE

In a cozy cafe on a winter's day
I sit with a steaming cup of hot chocolate
Rich and velvety, sweet and warm
It warms my hands and soothes my soul

The chocolate melts on my tongue
Sending waves of comfort through my body
I close my eyes and savor the moment
As the world slows down around me

Each sip is like a gentle hug
A moment of pure bliss in a hectic world
I breathe in the aroma of cocoa
And let the sweetness fill me up

Hot chocolate, a simple pleasure
A reminder to slow down and enjoy
In a world that moves too fast
It's the little things that bring the most joy.

THE ART OF SPRING

In the dance of spring,
nature reveals its artistry
The world awakens
from its wintry slumber
Colors burst forth
from every corner
Life breathes anew
in the warm sunshine

Leaves unfurl
to greet the gentle breeze
Flowers bloom in a riot of hues
Birds sing
their joyful melodies
As the earth comes alive
with the promise of growth

In the art of spring,
we witness the beauty
As Mother Nature weaves
her masterpiece
into the fabric of the season
A symphony of rebirth
that never fails to captivate
our hearts and minds.

THE SONG OF SUMMER

In the lazy afternoon haze,
The song of summer plays
A melody of warmth and light,
A symphony of colors bright.

The humming of the bees,
The rustling of the trees,
The laughter of children at play,
The perfect end to a summers day.

The sun dips low in the sky,
Painting the clouds with a fiery dye,
And as the day fades into night,
The song of summer takes flight.

It whispers of lazy days spent,
Of memories made and time well-vent,
A reminder of the joys that pass,
But leave behind a lasting gasp.

So let the music of summer sing,
And let its melody take wing,
For in its song we find,
The beauty of all things kind.

THE DANCE OF AUTUMN

In the stillness of the autumn air,
Leaves cascade in a graceful dance,
An elegant ballet of red and gold,
Nature's masterpiece in trance.

The trees sway to a gentle rhythm,
A symphony of rustling leaves,
Whispering secrets of the season,
A spectacle that never ceases to please.

Golden sunlight filters through,
Creating a magical haze,
As the Earth prepares for slumber,
In the waning days of autumn's phase.

The dance of autumn is a sight to behold,
A fleeting moment of beauty and grace,
A reminder of life's ever-changing ways,
In this tranquil season, we find solace.

THE SLUMBER OF WINTER

In the quiet of winter's slumber,
The world blanketed in white,
Nature takes a peaceful rest,
Under the cold, starry night.

The trees stand tall and bare,
Their branches reaching high,
As the frost settles gently,
And the snowflakes softly fly.

The animals hibernate,
In their cozy, warm abode,
Dreaming of spring's return,
As they sleep beneath the cold.

The Earth lies still and silent,
In the grip of winter's hold,
But beneath the frozen surface,
Life begins to unfold.

For even in the darkest season,
There is beauty to be found,
In the slumber of winter's embrace,
Peace and tranquility abound.

Coffee Season

THOSE WHO ROAM . VIII

ROAMING STREETS

In the city streets I roam,
A wanderer in search of home.
The neon lights flicker and glow,
As I walk these streets alone.

The busy hustle and bustle,
Of people rushing here and there.
But in the midst of it all,
I find a sense of solace and care.

The buildings tower above me,
Their shadows casting a protective gaze.
I feel the weight of history,
In these streets where memories blaze.

Each corner turned brings a new surprise,
A hidden gem waiting to be found.
I'm a nomad in this urban jungle,
With adventures yet unbound.

So I'll keep roaming these streets,
Exploring every alley and avenue.
For in the heart of the city,
I find myself, reborn anew.

AWAY FROM HOME, LET'S ROAM

In the lands unknown, let's roam
Far from the comfort of home
Let's roam.
Across mountains and fields we'll ponder
Exploring what lies yonder
Let's roam.
Through forests dense and wide
Let's embrace the feeling of being untied
To any place or time constraint
As we wander without restraint
Let's roam.
In the stillness of a foreign shore
We'll find solace in the unfamiliar lore
And in the vast expanse of sky above
We'll feel the freedom of uncharted love
Let's roam.
So let's journey far, hand in hand
Away from the safety of our familiar land
Embracing the thrill of the great unknown
As we wander, together, not alone
Let's roam.

OCEAN RAOMERS

In the depths of the ocean, a diver braves
A world beneath the waves
Majestic creatures swim around
Tranquility in the sound

The diver moves with grace and skill
Exploring the coral hill
Sunlight filters through the blue
Revealing a world so new

Mysterious and unknown
In this underwater zone
The ocean diver is at peace
Surrounded by the ocean's cease

A world of wonder and awe
Beneath the ocean's raw
The diver explores with wonder
In this world down under

So here's to the ocean diver
A brave and curious explorer
In the depths where few may roam
Finding beauty in the ocean's home.

Coffee Season

SWITZERLAND

Coffee Season

IN THE HEART OF SWITZERLAND

In the heart of Europe lies a land of pristine beauty
Where snow-capped mountains reach for the sky
And crystal-clear lakes reflect the azure heavens above
This is Switzerland, a paradise on Earth.

The rolling hills are dotted with quaint villages
Where time seems to stand still in peaceful pause
The sound of cowbells echoes through the valleys
A symphony of nature's harmonious song.

In the cities, like Zurich and Geneva
The spirit of innovation thrives and prospers
As bustling streets buzz with the energy of progress
Yet the ancient charm of history lingers in every corner

The Swiss are proud and noble people
Their traditions and culture woven into the fabric of their land
A dedication to excellence in all they do
From chocolate to watches, their craftsmanship is unmatched...

next ...

... continued

... And oh, the beauty of the Swiss Alps
Majestic and grand, a playground for adventurers
Skiing in the winter, hiking in the summer
A paradise for those who seek the thrill of the unknown.

Switzerland, a land of peace and prosperity
Where the air is fresh and the waters pure
A haven for those who seek refuge from the chaos of the world
In this paradise called Switzerland, where dreams come true.

THE ALPS

Among the rolling hills and valleys,
Where the heaves touch the Earth,
There lies a majestic beauty,
A sight of unmatched worth.

The Alps stretch high into the sky,
Their peaks crowned with snow,
A timeless symbol of nature's power,
A wonder to behold.

Each mountain tells a story,
Of battles fought and won,
Of conquerors and explorers,
Whose journey had just begun.

The valleys are filled with life,
Flowers blooming in the meadows,
Streams flowing down the slopes,
A symphony of nature's echoes...

··· next

... continued

... As the sun sets behind the peaks,
Painting the sky in shades of pink,
The Alps seem to come alive,
A living, breathing link.

To a world so pure and untouched,
A sanctuary for the soul,
A place where one can find peace,
And feel truly whole.

So let us raise a toast,
To the Alps so grand and tall,
A treasure beyond compare,
A wonder for us all.

Coffee Season

french vanilla . IX

Coffee Season
FRENCH VANILLA

In a quaint French cafe

On a warm summer day

I sip on a cup of French Vanilla

The creamy sweetness lingers

On my lips and fingertips

As I savor each decadent sip

The rich aroma fills the air

A comforting embrace

As I lose myself in the taste

Of this beloved French delicacy

The smoothness of the vanilla

Dances on my tongue

A symphony of flavors

That leaves me feeling young

I close my eyes and breathe

Taking in the essence

Of this comforting indulgence

French vanilla, oh how you delight

In every moment, day or night

I'll always hold you close

In my hear, where you belong

So here's to you, French vanilla

A treat for the senses

A taste of bliss

Forever cherished in my soul.

BIRDS FILL THE AIR

Birds fill the air
With their melodious song
Each note a gift
From their delicate lungs

Their feathers glisten
In the golden light
As they dance on the wind
So graceful in flight

They soar through the heavens
With a message of peace
A reminder to us all
That freedom will never cease

Their symphony of chirps
A soothing lullaby
A gentle reminder
Of beauty in the sky

So let us cherish
These winged creatures rare
For they bring joy and wonder
As they fill the air.

SUMMER DREAMS

In the hazy days of summer dreams,
We find ourselves immersed in golden light,
Lulled by the lapping waves and gentle breeze,
Our cares melt away in the heat of the night.

Bare feet on hot sand, a cool drink in hand,
The world feels so still, so perfectly right,
As fireflies dance and stars twinkle above,
We are lost in this moment, in pure delight.

Memories are made in these lazy days,
Of laughter and love, of joy and play,
We hold onto them tightly, like treasures untold,
In the warmth of summer, our dreams unfold.

AUTUMN BLUES

In the crisp air of autumn,
I feel a sense of melancholy,
As the leaves turn gold and fall,
I can't help but feel a sense of loss.

The days grow shorter,
The nights grow colder,
And I can't shake this feeling,
Of longing and sadness.

Autumn blues settle in my soul,
A reminder of endings,
And the inevitable decay of time,
But I find solace in the beauty,
Of the changing seasons,
And the promise of new beginnings,
That lie just beyond the horizon.

THE BIG CHILL

The big chill of winter
Creeps in on whispered winds
Tucking us in with its icy fingers
And painting the world in shades of white

Frosty breath hangs in the air
As we huddle closer for warmth
The trees stand stripped bare
Their branches reaching out in desperation

Yet there is beauty in this cold
A stillness that calms the soul
A time to slow down and reflect
To find peace in the midst of the storm

So let the big chill of winter
Wrap you in its icy embrace
And remind you that even in darkness
There is always a glimmer of light.

Coffee Season

THOSE WHO ROAM . IX

TRAVEL SQUAD

In a world where paths diverge
And hearts long for new horizons
There lies a bond unbreakable
Forged on dusty roads and foreign skies

Our travel squad, a ragtag bunch
Of wanderers and dreamers bold
We seek adventure, never knowing
Where our next journey will unfold

Through laughter shared and tears shed
We find our spirits intertwined
For in each other's company
Our souls are truly aligned

We roam the world, a fearless tribe
Exploring lands both near and far
United by our love for travel
And the beauty found in every star

So here's to us, my travel squad
May our journey's never end
For in each other's presence
Our hearts forever blend.

CLIFF DIVE

On the edge of surrender
Nerves tingling with fear
Heart pounding with anticipation
The edge of the cliff calls out

A leap of faith awaits
In the open expanse of blue
The wind whispers sweet nothings
As I prepare to take the plunge

I close my eyes
And let go of all my doubt
Feeling weightless
As I soar through the air

The water rushes up to meet me
Cool and inviting
A moment of freedom
In the midst of chaos

I resurface
Breathless and exhilarated
The cliff jump may be over
But the memory lingers on.

THE CAVE

In the depths of the Earth
There lies a hidden place
A sanctuary of shadows

Where the darkness dances
And the silence hums
A mysterious rhythm

Echoes of ancient whispers
Haunt the cavern walls
Carrying secrets untold

This is The Cave
A place of solitude
A gateway to the soul

So step into the darkness
Embrace the mystery within
And let The Cave reveal

The depths of your being
And the light that shines
In the shadows of your heart.

Coffee Season

OH CANADA!

MAPLE SYRUP

In the heart of the forest
Amidst the towering trees
There lies a sweet treasure
Made by the busy bees

Maple syrup, golden and pure
A gift from nature's hand
Drizzling down pancakes
In distant lands

From the tapping of the trees
To the boiling of the sap
Each step taken with care
To create this sweet trap

The taste is rich and bold
A flavor that's hard to beat
Drizzled on waffles and ice cream
A culinary feat

So here's to maple syrup
A sweet and sticky delight
A taste of nature's goodness
That brings joy with every bite.

CANADIAN POUTINE

In the land of maple leaves and snowy peaks
There lies a dish that truly speaks
Of comfort, warmth, and cheesy delight
Poutine, the Canadian culinary delight.

Crispy fries, golden and hot
Topped with cheese curds, melted on the spot
And smothered in gravy, rich and thick
This dish is sure to satisfy the pickiest critic.

A symphony of flavors, a decadent treat
Poutine is a dish you won't soon forget
It warms the soul on a cold winter's night
And brings a smile to your face at first sight.

So let us raise a fork, dig in with glee
To this humble dish that brings happiness
Poutine, the comfort food we all adore
A taste of Canada, forevermore.

BEAVER TAILS

In the heart of Canada, a sweet delight
The beaver tail, a tasty treat made just right
Deep-fried dough, sprinkled with sugar and spice
A perfect indulgence, a Canadian paradise

Shaped like the tail of our furry friend
Crunchy on the outside, soft within
Served piping hot, a comforting pleasure
A local favorite, a national treasure

From Ottawa to Vancouver, they are adored
A delicious snack, never to be ignored
So if you find yourself in the Great White North
Be sure to try a beaver tail, for all it's worth.

SASKATOON BERRY PIE

In the heart of the prairies
Where the wild Saskatoon berries grow
There's a sweetness that fills the air
A taste of home, a memory to share

Gathered in the early light
Plump a ripe, a purplish hue
Whispering secrets of the land
Whispering stories, old and new

Baked into a flaky crust
With sugar and spice to enhance
The Saskatoon berry pie emerges
A delight for every sense

Juicy and tart, a perfect blend
Of flavors that dance on the tongue
A taste of summer in every bite
A taste of the prairies, forever young

So let us gather around the table
With friends and family by our side
To savor the Saskatoon berry pie
A taste of home, a joyful ride.

BANNOCK

Upon the hearth, the dough is placed
A staple of the indigenous race
Mixing flour and water with care
Creating a treat so simple and rare

Bannock, oh Bannock, so warm and sweet
A comfort food that can't be beat
Grilled or fried, it's deliciously cooked
An age-old recipe that can't be overlooked

Pioneers and settlers alike
Enjoyed this treat, yet full of flavor
Bannock is a dish we will always savor

Bannock, oh Bannock, a symbol of tradition
A reminder of our ancestral nutrition
A dish that brings people together
Sharing stories and memories that will last forever.

Other Books Written by the Author

POETRY

. Coffee Season
(NOW AVILABLE)

. Dance In the Rain (Haiku's)
. Love Letter's From Japan
. Soul Food
. Love Stories from the Heart
(COMING SOON)

CHILDREN'S BOOKS

. Toshi and the missing Ball-y
. Toshi visits London, England
. Toshi visits Pairs, France
. Toshi in Tokyo
. Toshi and his human sisters

NOVELS

. The Kingdom of Arundel Series Books
(COMING SOON)

A Note on the Author

Dina Ezzeddine is a writer and illustrator from Canada. Dina has a degree in Visual Arts and Design, as well as a Bachelor of Arts degree in English. Dina has written numerous children's book and numerous teen books. This book of poetry is her latest work. You can find more of Dina's upcoming work online!

Find more of Dina's here:
visit Amazon & IngramSpark

----

author_illustratordina
aiko10195@gmail.com

Extract from upcoming book
Dance In the Rain
Japanese Haiku's

TOKYO PRINCESS

Elegant Princess
In Tokyo's bustling streets
Graceful as cherry blossoms

OSAKA I MISS YOU

Gentle cherry blooms
Whispers of Osaka's charm
Longing in my heart

KYOTO TEMPLES

Cherry blossoms bloom
Kyoto memories linger
Peaceful temple grounds

Available on Amazon

www.ingramcontent.com/pod-product-compliance
Lightning Source LLC
Chambersburg PA
CBHW070429010526
44118CB00014B/1971